Praise for

FUTURE BOTANIC

Christina Olivares is a sonic soothsayer on the page, yes! Olivares loves lush language and liminal space and has returned to the page with a curious ferocity for softness among the rubble. In *Future Botanic*, Olivares studies the archives of lineage, community, and her own body. Each poem an altar offering, each line break an ancestor's relinquishing. This collection is a spectrum of girl bliss and gender, concrete gardens and blood conjure, and is a spiritually (re)evolutionary promise. The "botanical no-américa, inverse" survives and revives us all.

—Mahogany L. Browne, author of
I Remember Death by Its Proximity to What I Love and *Vinyl Moon*

In *Future Botanic* Olivares writes, "... the Bronx is a spell on us that we also make." Olivares is such a beautiful caster of spells that as readers we are transfixed by something beyond language—which, stunning in its own right, is still a slow second to her primal landscapes—her blossomed imagery. This collection succeeds in rooting itself in many spaces, queer and exact in its belonging and estrangement. "Imagine yourself free, safe and loved"—Olivares is a world builder without limits—her radical imagination, her keen seeing a blanket for hiding, for warmth, for living after liberation—

—Yesenia Montilla, author of
The Pink Box and *Muse Found in a Colonized Body*

Whereas José Martí left Cuba for New York and imagined a hemispheric
America that bridged North and South, Christina Olivares summons
"a botanical / no-américa" that is neither north nor south but rather "botanic
imaginings" of how "our américa built itself inside of us." *Future Botanic*
is a dissident queer love song to "this dirt of the américas," from the
ancestors' journey from Cuba to Harlem, to a Bronx housing project, to the
touch of a lover's hand, to the dead we carry with us and the infinite desires
and dreams burbling just below "our lit tongues." Words here are compressed
into prose blocks or unspool on the page in flowing tercets that reveal a
restless, genderless mind traveling inward to where the "I" is "a blade / of
unused womb." For Olivares, writing is a diasporic act of naming the violences
of empire (and our complicity with them); she insists on poetry as a radically
speculative practice of summoning "our multiversed futurities," and we are
lucky to have such a healing ecology of language: "For the seeds we are, fed
on dreaming."

—Urayoán Noel, author most recently of
Transversal, and 14 collections of poetry, prose, and translations

FUTURE BOTANIC

C. Olivares

Get Fresh Publishing, A Non-Profit Corp.
PO Box 901
Union, NJ 07083

www.gfbpublishing.org

ISBN: 9798218120108

Library of Congress Control Number: 2023931120

Cover, layout, typesetting, and design:
culture glut llc
cultureglut.com

Proofreading and editorial:
Ann W. Hagerty

Back cover photo of vines by Ananda Lima

Front cover: Art installation by Gabriela Salazar, *Matters in Shelter (Displacement)*, 2018.
Concrete blocks, coffee clay, (used coffee grounds, flour, salt). 17 x 17 x 60.
Photo of installation by Katrina Neumann

This book was typeset in Built Titling & Bembo Std.

We must now collectively undertake a rewriting of knowledge as we know it.

—Sylvia Wynter

Contents

INHERITANCE TRIPTYCH

Girl

After the burnings,
the lots were our inheritance. We exploded
green from soil flush with rubber, shredded plastics,

concrete, metal, glass. Nightly we stood under showers
while dreaming shadows dislodged and fled
down the drain. We knew we'd begun in her some mystery

also begun in ourselves. The killings we did,
just to see: pinch up a white-rooted sprout, flecked
in soil, then squeeze till threads dissolve into wet

wetness, milk, as milk as dirt. I wanted labor,
fruit and excess. To know, to know. To rear the self
taken root—a queer, livid coiling that couldn't be

bludgeoned or picked apart. A demanding love, drawing
circles on my chest with a muddy finger, earth a muddy
finger on my tongue, as thoroughly confounded as me.

The rain: cold splashy kisses, warm needling kisses.
The garden? A cosmos, burned, then turned over in palms
till it came unburned. A girl's body

readying itself. Eventually the dirt we are is returned
to us for reaping. A kick against extinction, to imagine
closeness where there is only other. We left a wake of wings

on our threshing floor.

Portrait

        of one of us: small girl in a messy dress,
the sleeve is pink as a tongue, jacaranda-jeweled tree

an imagined fire beside. What

is left behind is never
left behind if we never
     disown its weight

                     Let her   and her press
                 her body here   and there

you might become any burned house
an open palm upon which your future ghosts will cut
astonished rivers

           Everything, and yearning, might snag
                        sing

                  in your current
You might

become night, a succession of her and her mouths,
lucid. A hot swift. A starling
startling northward.   Lonely

    but good,

      you're so good that when clouds
          open over Fordham Road you
                  turn mythical

turn into a palomita and rise, rise into

smoke, seed-scattered,

a child's daydream: *am I becoming, have I become*

Plot

Nobody ever said, direct like that, *You can't love girls*
like you. But I knew. Overspilled and luscious, how disgraceful.

Slough this body. Mock it clean. Lop it, lick it, prune it clean. Sinuous,
vestigial bluff of a body, contempt flowered this body

wet with fear, wet with shame, every cell wet, a whole condition
that alchemizes into freedom if you

don't die from it first. I know to be embodied in any américa
is to be ruined by violence, and wow how many forms does its violence

take. The second person I ever loved taught me delight,
lay me in a bordered plot, and when she saw me, marveled,

whispered into my ear: *You are just like me.*

OUR AMÉRICA IS BOTANIC

sparrows jam sneakers
thrown over a telephone line
with nests   at dusk

                                        we're crowded
                                        in a back seat, dirt-funky
                                        playing the quiet

        game   we break when we spy
        mcdonald's, glow singing us singing
        back as a lady in front wavers high

                        high high: it's always apocalypsing
                                apocalypso—riddled earthbody tilts

                                as it sprouts us

for this home land,
this américa
unpracticed parent,

                unparalleled lover

and slowly, one summer,

      two summers, gliding to three,

                we conjure a real garden

        from this rubbled lot   like

sprout
     lit

        small grasses waving

    been on   fire or been left

alone to grow

              accidental, inconsequential

             echoes, ancestral/astral

        this tiny garden
          we wanted so bad

                lean out the windows, call

hey

                        hey

                                        hey

de- and re- compose

                our green
                        this swollen green
        our milky/murky   our studied shoots
bleaked on sky

summer/stunners
        before the city

                                decades later

                                        rich again

wants it back

On a yellow bus, our young gods instructed: *sit up front*. Small thing in feet that don't touch a floor, tracing my finger along the breath-patterned glass with growing fire in my belly as neighborhoods zip past more and more familiar until they implode, dizzily, joyfully, into the zenith of my own. When we park for our field trip I tell my teacher *that's where I live* and point toward the lofty grey building above us, its squat windows, its apartment letters painted on the outside, its face full of camera eyes. She's blank, instructs me inside. On the way out I try again. Her blankness meets me a second time: I see it fix itself inside her, blossom. I see the trouble is my botanical talk, little claws, what my home is.

       Upwind factory churns burnt and sweet. We always want cookies, especially in the summer when the windows are open and we're lazy with heat. Our young god gathers me up to read poem after poem for her homework. They all talk Spanish over our heads. A cousin says *ax* instead of *ask* but I'm not allowed to. Summer marked by the garden, the sun marveling us, this itchy wanting, for cookies, for our skin to burst us into glitter. *She had horses who danced in her mother's arms. / She had horses who thought they were the sun and their / bodies shone and burned like stars.* I sneak into the kitchen to scale the countertop for sweets tin-sealed on the fridge. She scolds: *don't touch the oven. —it ain't even on. —isn't.*

                    how

                        don't
                        can
                        do

                            we imagine

                            ourselves?

that summer I dreamt a pony at the door
and I woke up
                            young hands poking

in the dusked light squared
                            above and so eagerly

wishing, wishing, wishing

                            I check, skidding on thready socks,
                            all want

What's a pony to a girlchild in the projects?
a regurgitated dream?
a fever-dream of your best girl self?
Beautiful, hot to the touch,
unoriginal?   Can you
be good enough for one
to appear for you—first you, then
the dream of the queer animal you are
afraid to be, such good,
good girls both?

I say the Bronx burned but

       what I'm sure of is only that
       we ate its earth as children   a transfer of desiring
       it to us   us to it

       silky-threaded little bodies   plus
       burned land's milky sustaining   reassembling
       making itself new again in our
       little new bodies

a queer love song:

       our américa built itself inside of us   a botanical
       no-américa, inverse that survived   made-new

our américa   our knowledges are
                     seeds carefully folded in our dirt-
                     soaked little hands
                     given

                              given over to each other

our américa   a fever
dream edging delight

                                                        thickly
                                     renders us

infrastructure
carceral
schools
work no work
violence turned on us
turned inward

our américa

          coiling and lush,

                    papered over in dead-myths,

                              alive, kicking under the surface,
our américa

                    just out of sight

                                        botanical
                                        livewire

how does dirt remember me?
what ecology does it make of my body, tasting it?

a floral-florid botanic body, a child
cut of patterned patchwork earth—assess inheritance

by tracing the blooms down your arms,
the horse-language of your body, your dense thighs and

your loudest laugh

assess inheritance by noting

joy of cousins,
baby brother

My brother and I drag trembly-legged, waxed-wood
kitchen chairs. In deep August you can smush their
skins like a membrane. In the winter you can flake their
wax into crescent fingernails. From them we watch the
sun set above the river and the bridge, above cars or
guns or fireworks popping, evil and breathlessly
wanting the tiny boats filled with the college rowers
who wear opaque suits over their strong limbs and
whose young gods have never warned them *don't touch
that water* to capsize into what we conjure below: a toxic
aquarium festooned with the dead and tires and tiny
bags full of hastily chucked drugs and sacks full of old
money and broken records flags bullets burnt-out cars
and children's tutus and paired shoes strung over also-
sunken phone wires and concrete foundations for houses
that were never built and three-eyed fish, water glowing
cleaner and quieter the deeper they fall, clear to some
other side nobody, not even us playing, can see. What
our young gods did not/could not teach us: how to sew
ourselves into the varied earths of the other world. What
use in that other américa is our spit, what spells to put
into the water jars on the windowsill and under which
light to protect against our erasure. How tender we are,
want to be, avoid being, try to be. How to dress a wound
and send it out into that world to be. Does the heart
weigh more out there or less. Our bones, spilling. The
difference between myth and memory and how spelling
figures. How to remember all our names and places.
How to not fall into the river. That the Bronx is a spell
on us which we also make.

(back in our garden)

—our desire to find the astonishing,
be astonishing ourselves,

sprout, needle, confusing excess of our skin,

the rain we, yelling and delighted, our drenched mouths opening
like small vises, know is acid,

transforming us into
superheroes, our lit tongues
neon with candy

our cousin's finger taps the soil lightly to make a finger-shaped hollow

     inside the hollow she puts things we are made of
     her cheek is streaked in cheez doodle dust

she activates its archive
with bits of water, glitter rounding
drop by drop off her hand,

               us all

               dreaming

of the next,
even as our next
is unimaginable
to us

UPTOWN SUMMERS

Lexington & 110th. I sit carefully on the lap of a person I love. T. walks over, she is alive, she touches my arm as she laughs through a story. The sun pushes all of the color into her eyes. Sumptuous, ours, time unfolds in negative. To think I almost didn't come today because I couldn't figure out what to wear. Cookout smoke unspools above the parking lot, sunlight slants off the windows—buildings turn riotous, orange, darkly purple-fired. Our squeaky folding chair bearing us bearing us.

Fire sheets the southeast corner of 125th and Lenox
in thin ghosts, waves twice as high
as the squat, splintering row it's chosen. Smoke laps

our eyes, noses, ululates into the mouth
of the subway. A blockful of live ash suspended
in the air, in us. I'm beside two older men, the three of us marveling

from an unsafe distance. Traces settle on our faces.
Lone NYPD loops long circles on the far street.
No fire trucks. In a different story, I'd write—

evenly they coiled
the yellow hose
evenly they doused the fire.

At home, I don't wash my hair right away. If I hold it on my body,
it happened. Earlier this winter, licking batter
off a spoon, I saw an empty building catch fire,

its top floor windows exploding in tight pops
over 123rd. That time the trucks did come, irradiating
night. Disasters verify what we're taught

or try to forget: low and foamy as a lullaby,
everything is always singing
its ending song.

It's midnight, a different year, and we're home early, girls rolling and climbing, limb over wet limb, into a tiny shower on the thirteenth floor. Only the projects in this city have a thirteenth floor. Tomorrow it'll be early morning, and light pouring over the river will wake us up—pancakes or chicken for breakfast in the red-walled kitchen. For now we fit our bodies into one bed to sleep. In the afternoon we'll duct-tape plastic wrap to the linoleum, pour dish soap in a long thin ribbon from hallway to the edge of the living room, swish water with bare hands and feet, and we'll have a slip 'n slide. Spread my palms across one friend's collarbone, her shoulder blades, mimic wings. Another combs the sorrow out of my wet hair with her fingers. Death is everywhere! We turn our secrets over in awe! How dare we be so free.

We lose our loves, are gentrified out.
We dance:

dressed top to toe
in Black,
          adorned

                    in lilac butterfly wings—a Brown boy
                    gone rogue in shimmer, threading
                    us, circling and circling

the round bar in the middle
of No Parking's dance
floor.

                                             We win, we win.
                                   Insistent
                                        fucking alive. We drank
of this earth we are?
               We choose to love the dirt
                              we are?   We drank

of our sound
               that rings between us, glints of light
                              we burn and give?

Found
        that this living

                    is for joy?

RETURN

Queer twist of the américas—

bloqueo,

                                                    embargo

          committing to paper

what I learn in Spanish   in English.

                                          My youngest self

                    first landing in Havana twenty years ago—

Vedado. At a tertulia, an artist sells cuadros, listed in rows on lace that's been unrolled over a twin-sized bed. He asks my name. He tells me my great-grandfather was a doctor and a mayor and cured him of a difficult illness in childhood. *I see him in you—you look just like him,* he says, radiant with generosity, holding my hands, touching my cheek, which is wet now too. *Such a good man—you are so blessed. Such a very good man—welcome home.*

Guantanamo. A girl unrolls a cloth to sell candy in the shade. I've carried a handmade map on this trip to the intersection where *the good man* lived once upon a time, patriarch of this family home. Neighbors warn me this tío abuelo I'm searching for is fundido. I am a time-space traveler, so we are uniquely suited to meet. I feed him pictures of our family through the door, and he accepts me, leads me across our broken threshold, grasping my wrist lightly in an o.

No bricks, mortar, steel beams, concrete blocks, iron, planks of whole wood or glass available during the week I stay, so we construct language instead. We wander through the house he's mutilated. He shows me the town, the library that houses his favorite librarian, best cheese sandwiches, his sitting bench. I ask a lot of questions. He unearths scraps of paper to write spells, prescriptions, recipes: on one, piña; on another, a string of numbers; a third, a sketched dog with mathematical equations for limbs. My favorite part of the house, of which very little isn't stripped, sold, or stolen, is a limbed, twisty tree in the courtyard. At the entrance, a family portrait is fixed to the wall so firmly it can't be removed. I trace the shape of my posture, mouth, eyes, in the postures, mouths, eyes on the wall.

I am in New York when he passes. The restrictions in place make it too complex and costly to cross. A person I love goes to Puerto Rico at the same time and upon my request finds young flowers and lays them in the sea at night to drift outward toward the point of light on the horizon that is him.

Viñales. La ceiba florece cada tres años. Inside the seed is something that looks like a ball of cotton. When the ceiba last flowered, the seed and spun sugar inside drifted over the whole valley like snow. This man leading me on a nature walk insists there is no racism in Cuba and also differentiates white norteaméricanos as *puro* and Black and Brown norteaméricanos as *de color,* asking with genuine confusion, *95% de las personas que vienen de tú país son de color. Porqué?* Cuba exports itself as a deracialized panacea. A life apart from norteamérican racism. Even the imagining—ghost of what could be, unmade seed of another reality—is a nourishment.

Toc toc toc. Viñales, years later. An official enters, says I'm a journalist. It's my typing, or I've made friends with the wrong stranger. Now the kind family renting me a room is frightened that I've lied on my visa, meticulously copied into their record book, which lists me as a tourist and not a journalist. No more buses out tonight. I promise I'll go in the morning. Sit on a roof, close to a slip of waxing moon not yet bright enough to streak these hills. A mangy kitten snoozes in my lap. One of their children leaves an espresso in a teacup, which I find, cold, hours later.

The official is almost right. Gather what's shared carefully as recipes, spells, fallen fruit. Before I learn how often it gets me followed, I like to tell people my surname. In a bluish *máquina*, the *taxista* answers with predictable astonishment. *—Adinerado? Moreno? Del oriente?* before he gifts me a story.

Be a ready tree, a ready ground, a ready wind, a sheeting rain. To break open at the point of contact. Sometimes others want this too. Wait, open, listen. Take up small space so the rest fills with story. Anonymize and anachronize notes, create an archive of soundings and relations, protected by its unverifiability if ever taken during a border search.

Then, November 2016. *—La isla? Una cárcel. —Che? Un asesíno.*

In July it takes hours to find Cristál beer. This tío abuelo—cream linen, polished wood cane, gold on gold. We walk slow to be seen. In this heat that quivers and licks your lungs, that pressures your temples, this beer, the plastic chairs we slide into, is the best, the best. He asks about you, Zachary, asks again and then more. Later we look at old family photos in his apartment, dark and cool while the radio chirps.

During my first visit, this tío abuelo threw a tertulia to celebrate my return. I learned a place had been set and held to slip into. In pictures I'm stunned, thawing. He's sometimes in frame, sometimes just an elbow. During my last visit, I meet his wife, my tía abuela, declaiming erotic poetry in their kitchen. Two or three nights before she passes, I dream of her, intend to call, wave lit incense out the window instead, holding out, as always, too lightly and too long. She leaves us at the start of the pandemic. He in 2022. For him, I drift flowers outward in another part of nuestro caribe, toward the light he is, which is all light, everywhere, the boats flickering, the satellites, the uncrushed moon, the uncrushed stars, each of our unreturned.

In her kitchen, she'd instructed:

Be unafraid.
Learn the theater
of the poem.
Live the theater
of the poem
so when you open your mouth
you become
what you've made.
There is no separation
between who you are
what you say
and what it's made of you.

I dream of gold-tía abuela, barefoot,

barefoot, a girl
on the dusty   *brow of shore, the wind rushes*

        in a swell
to meet you   *to carry your*
                          fleet-foot forward

you wear
the thin lace dress—
                    a loose-threaded sheath
                          over your breastbone

        your mother
made, you wear   *the women*
                    who made you, all of them,

            you are wearing
the women   *the women are*   *a flag*
                    and you

are running
                    you are running in the narrow

flat sand

        you are running
        into headwind

                    you are a girl

                      headed home

Back home in New York, I am gentled by abuela, our Sunday dinners that must contain one meat, her atomic storytelling. What happens fifty years after you leave your homeland? She wears those chanclas with netting dotted in iridescent plastic leaves, mimicking flowers, the ones they sell for over a dollar at the dollar store in every bold or soft color. She lives in a part of Harlem that Cubans here nicknamed El Escambray. When the first—since 1959—commercial flights from the US to Havana start, I needle her: look it's so easy, they say we can buy tickets online. Don't you wanna go? —*No, no, no.*

Imaginative failure as protection means—don't believe something could be so don't prepare for when it becomes. After years of traveling strangely, or not traveling at all, JetBlue goes: You're ready to jet! A string of confirming letters appears and—as if resetting bones—pain. Generational trauma made me stupid. Thinking on this narrow flight path—destroyed by empire, reinstituted by empire—that the family causeway you are tracing isn't your own, that you're somehow exempt, intact, sovereign. *No, no, no.*

Always I carry some letter to protect me. Employer, school, nonprofit, another poet, whoever's. Three kinds of cash, not including dollars. A norteamérican passport, which we're not allowed to put in the microwave or hammer snitch-free.

Fidel's Cuba, dream that it is, frees me to dream. I learn that if I am not careful, I will reflexively live out the dreams—hierarchy, loneliness, acquisition—of these invented américas that I did not make but insist over my imagining. Choose which to keep, which to use as salve, which to crack open, which to burn. Fidel's Cuba, dream that it is, fucked up my family: dissident, queer, scientist, artist. Some in my family witnessed the revolution's executions, friends, neighbors, lining streets. Others in my family drew the lists, made the orders, ascended the ranks. Piece the story together in tertulias, máquinas, entranceways, fields, backyards, cafés, bars, bookstores, classrooms, kitchens, buses, attics, but it stays full of holes, bullets and otherwise.

First visit. We sit in folding chairs around uneven tables. Assata Shakur enters after her security checks us out. She asks us to each tell her our name and a hope for the future. We do. She listens to us one by one. She makes of us the opposite of nation: infinite sound, as many listenings. She takes us the next night to a tertulia in Vedado with strangers, where a child in a gauzy dress plays a violin. There is hardly any food and so much to drink. An artist who paints cuadros recognizes the face of a man he loved in my face. We grip each other and laugh and cry. I carry in my face the face of a man who healed a boy. This boy, now a painter, touches my cheek gently, the way a father might. My archive is this cheek, shape of this mouth, who knows what else.

A different man on a different horse in a different part of the island falls back and back until it's just us riding side by side, away from large groups of tourists far in front and behind us. This is how it happens: a taxista rolling up his windows to speak. A writer closing shutters and beckoning me into an inner room upstairs to speak. A florist bending into a thicket of infant trees, where I am kneeling, astonished at their blooming, close enough to speak. A waiter pretending to have a glass of water on a short break, leaning on a table close enough to speak. A woman who walks me into her garden, listening for a particular silence that will indicate the neighbors aren't watching, then turning her full attention on me to speak. And so on.

Out here, in this field, this rider who by now has deliberately lost our pack wants to tell me the penalties for crimes. I want to hear him. He lists them, repeating slowly until he is sure I understand. He repeats himself in the softest declamation the forms of state violence that boundary his life. Capturing a lobster. Bootlegging cigars. The death of a horse, a cow, oxen. I say: *Fucked.* He says: *Remember. Will you remember?* To remember is a deception. Holding a thing isn't changing or knowing a thing. But he understands this. He is not a ghost speaking to me who is also not a ghost. I also remember how hot the horse's body was under my thighs, how by noon the sun had cut us sharply into pieces. *Yes.*

That night I dream I catch a lobster with my bare hands. Four years in jail. It snaps in my fingers, in Santiago de Cuba, beyond where the oil barges rise from the glassy-eyed bay. I dream of a horse's mouth open with flies. Four more years in jail. I put his language in my lungs and stomach to hold for him. I smuggle it here, to norteamérica, where our dreaming is bounded by other violences.

A group of ballerinas has adopted me for the night. Everybody is a child of the américas here. We work it through in one tongue as we sweat it out in another, spectrals of light clotting the dance floor. CUC drinks. CUC snacks. A dancer says to me:

It must be lonely
in your [uds.] liberation struggle

to imagine
norteamérica is not part of las américas.

RADICAL IMAGINING
IS OUR EVOLUTIONARY
PROJECT

None of us have ever died

None of us die

None of us will ever die

a narrative redress

to haunting: embodied earth of me

meets embodied earth of you

Nation is complex inside of us. What is nation but blood. The bloods in me all make different noises. I belong to all the bloods in me. The shady unrested of mine who stir this dirt of the américas in circles with their fingers, who spit salt, oil, wind down my throat. Who comprise these cells. Who are nearly all the who of me. I do not know most of their names. They know most of mine, and they call me by them.

There aren't yet words to say
all the things we are now,

                in any of these words I know,

so hay que inventarlas. Make do
inventando, inventando!

          What do we trade off to live psychically intact?

Touch your finger long enough and steadily enough
and your nerves will stop registering your touch.

Walk into a field of violets and your sense of smell
will shut off: a field of violence, unrecorded.   In a poem,

that's a syntactical saturation.
          Lose a memory, and the memory
remains differently, and often as a felt thing: a haunting.

Understanding is an act of the imagination.
Archive blooms at points of touch between the self

and the archived.
      A seed or a body or an archive seals, stores, releases
information, instructions for its unfolding

and that unfolding is circumstantial because
whatever happens to it either allows for or changes

its outcome   prescribed by some past
it staggers into some future:

                    cómo se pronuncia *hijx*?

hijx (n.)—Child of these américas? Genderless and queer at root? Noted in a colonizing language, straddling english/spanish, singular and/or plural, unpronounceable either way. Make it up, make it up. Sound it out. Everyone breathing or once-breathing on the earth called the américas, which is all of the earth between the two poles in this hemisphere. Messed with by the dreams of these américas. Who participate and don't participate in its dreamings. Who reckon with our individual becomings and not-becomings within these américas. Who involuntarily blossom out from the dreamings that our ancestors—of or not of this—put hiddenaway in us. Who spend a lifetime rendering legible a self perceived by others through these américas' dreamings. All our built-up dissonances, resonances, generational, aggregating in us like spells, like cells. Who will be ingested by this earth and/or who have ingested this earth. Who are seeds and archives. Some parts of us irrecoverably erased. Some parts of us not yet evolved into being.

hijx (adj.)—Vibe of unrelenting disasters, dance-floor-hallowed, glistening unremarkably in this curious fold, a wrinkle of planetary memory? Luminous. Fruits fulla seeds, tiny, globular. Imagine this ransacked, dreamed-up hemispheric earth dreamed us up the same way it dreamed up dinosaurs, salt, soil, sea. Imagine we are its dream. Us: tiny calderos, our bodies holding and holding, remembering in pieces or not at all. Us: the dream-within-a-dream of these entire américas. How do stolen places sound in us, under us, bearing our weights. *No, no, no.* Dance it out, sound it out. Imagine this stolen earth still circles back to be the good dream in us. You suspect, maybe know all about your richness and chaos, little animal netted with dust from things that once held orbit, nettled with seeds of dreams that are us and beyond us. Us: tumbling, uterine future-holdings.

hijx (v.)—Living on a line—blurry and troubled—between dreaming and believing the dream is true. Walking dreams into existence. The ways we are killed, killing each other, picking the names of our passed-on safe and holding them under our tongues, deliberately and with such love archiving our holdings in our bodies. Locating our roots, the ones that give us our dreaming, bind us to the dreaming earth, to the dreams our other selves produced, here or elsewhere, to the dreams our future descendents will produce. Locating the roots within and choosing—if to keep. If to use as salve or to nourish. If to extricate and burn.

Heal or revision? What is to be free? Does the imagination fail short? How can we get free? Behave free? As a delusional state lethal to those it imagines other, what is any codified, embodied and enacted supremacy's antithesis? Antidote? How to unarchive this psychosis, this *profound neurosis,* the root turned on ourselves, on each other, from our bodies?

Imagine you are completely free, completely loved, and completely safe:

Everyone is, now:

Where or when does your imagination touch its limit?

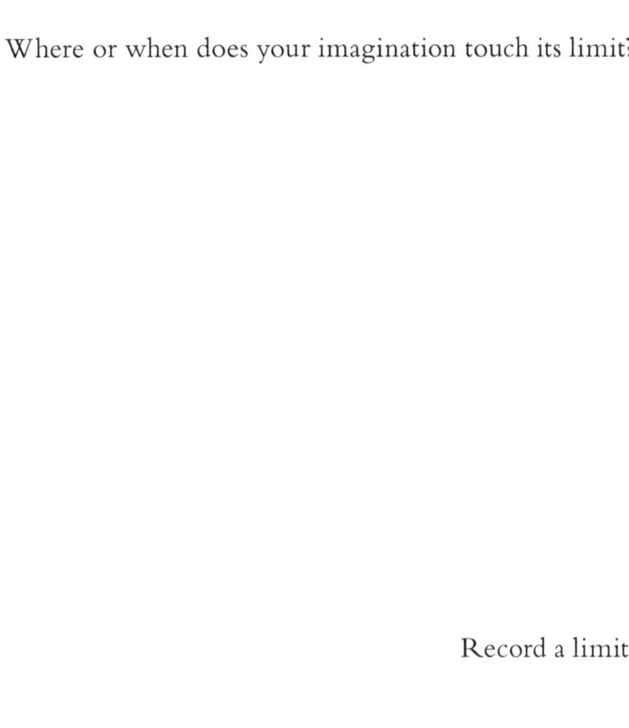

Record a limit:

Nourishment is

List, map, draw, say the unimaginable:

White supremacy, for example:

for a while it was hard to figure out what I was, in any américa.
I pass through customs lines undetectable as air. Cops don't stop me.
At work for the 1% I'm *thrown up against a sharp white background.*

A person of some color I loved used to call me halfbreed
—then one day delivers the punchline, laying our arms together:
halfbreed, you're browner than me.

The whitened body I am/am in is a dream
grinding against its own annihilation.   américa yearns
for my modification, enough whiteness, it thinks,

to take me as its own. Its courtship consists of withholding
more lethal forms of terrorism. I inventory my complicity.
I inventory it tomorrow, and the day after.

There aren't words in our languages
to say all the things we know or are, have become,
can trace ourselves to, run from, are claimed by.

Our men whitened children. Gradients arise from racial terror and also, at times, love, which is not always terror's antithesis. Casta painting 1:   . Casta painting 2:   . Casta painting 3:   . Casta painting 4: the baby sitting atop the mother's white? glisten legs, beside the father's glisten face, is Black. The painter affirms t/his continent's reality, which is, of course, a psychosis.

My imaginative failures—

little
and

catastrophic

what do my imaginative failures
protect?

Nourish the passed-on

Nourish the land

Nourish the descendants

anthropocene

redress:

lush
botanic
livewire

archive of griefs

becomes

submerged in stormwaters
dried out like flowers

pistil, stamen

feed the descendants
and the descendant land

failure of infrastructure

becomes

suitability of forged-in-violence américas

for thriving

one
baobab
seed
hidden
crossed
interred
twists up

outlasts the mill's

ruin

expands bright toward that sea

older

is of us

                                        radical imagining
                              is our evolutionary project
relinquishing our imaginative power
                   is the defeat

radical imagining
            is our evolutionary project
relinquishing our imaginative power
                    is the defeat

                                        radical imagining
                                      is our evolutionary project

                              relinquishing our imaginative
power
                        is the defeat

radical imagining is our evolutionary project

We become:

and then:

and then:

Imagine

          how the burned–clear
          songs

                   we invent

                         will keep us alive
                         will recode our cells

Imagine that you are an animal:

Imagine that you are the dream of the earth:

What does dirt dream?

DELIBERATELY AND WITH SUCH LOVE ARCHIVE THE HOLDINGS

Nepal, 2018; Harlem, 2016

1. *Traveling the Road to Manang over the River with Muna*

There is one road
into Manang. This Bolero,
one of a line of tiny Jeep-like Boleros,

etches spidery far below
and high above a sheer drop.
We track above

and beside the river. On the way to Manang
we ride against the current and up
and on the way from Manang

we ride with the current and down.
The light changes.
The landscape changes. Mist clings and blinks

and from a distance fixes hills
immobile. I think they are mountains
until days later, when Muna wakes

me up at dawn to show me
the real mountains—gold, stark, luminous,
human—before clouds soak in. The back is full of onions

on the verge. I learn all about Milarepa from a chatty monk en route
to his monastery. I fall in love with him, Milarepa.
Initially a vengeful mess, he gathers himself,

figures out the hard way how to mourn, love,
do better. Days later Muna will draw me by the hand into
a shop and select for me a Milarepa washed

in pale green
and bordered by embroidered cloth. His head
is cocked with a hand to his ear,   listening.   Muna's pressed

between the door and me. Our companion the monk
is pressed against the onions.
When we get stuck in the mud, he finds a patch

of pungent herbs that when burned wipe away
the smell of rot. We can't burn them in the car, so
he lays the torn stalks across the onion bags,

their skins split and paper
fluttered loose. We push free, continue on. The air begs lighter
and clearer the higher we go up.

I keep calling the black-green hills
mountains by accident. Day two:
We put on jackets. Blackened

chimneys sweeping starward, children,
small checkpoints—kiosks with men
inside, into which Muna disappears

and reappears. I feel worry
when she's out of sight. I am suspicious of men
but more so I lack object permanence. I play it cool

because she is cool, appearing, lifting herself easily into the cab,
handing me back my papers. An hour later
a waterfall blocks us, pooling deep and thrashing

over the edge of the road. Monsoon melts the road like
plastic, makes the road exactly what it is,
unsecured mud under water.

The men working on a new bridge
gesture exactly how to angle the tires to cross. On the way back
we learn a Bolero directly behind us slipped

off the edge. The driver broke both hands.
This first crossing, Muna holds
my hand. We ease down

into the pale torrent flanked by huge gray rocks.
The driver drives with surety. It is each of our lives
plus his livelihood on the line. The water drowns us a little,

rises to the window, spills in. He bounces us forward.
The water is pale blue,
pale stiff cold blue. I want to wash

my organs in its blue. I want
something rinsing to rise up and
pull us under, into its blue

violence. To locate its spray, softness
and float. We make it,
the way the living make it

and then forget how. Relief is exquisite
then fades. A little later, the road
is washed away again. Here, too, men

are building a bridge
that is only partially done. I reach for Muna's hand
before she reaches

for me, and we all plunge and survive again
together. I am not as frightened
as I should be, as I am when she walks into an empty

doorway alone or gets a
faraway look, but I amplify my fear
to give hers a home. We rise above one cloudline.

The mountains
are still obscured by some other
godlike cloudline, far. But sun beats hot, frantic

up here. Deep below,
in the fog, we can't see
the sun, which is there

the entire time, like the mountains.
The river dips and winks, far far below. Its glacier
is above Manang. The river higher and higher up is filled with stones

the size of eras, colored brilliant black
and clay. Its stones are what I would like to be,
a gray-black river boulder softened

under a never-ending cut of water.
The glacier that feeds this river
is clear, and Muna and I will hike toward it

soon, the morning after we walk
through Manang before dinner,
our gritty cold palms spinning

the rows of prayer wheels,
in the blue-black dusk that falls so quickly
we lose ourselves in the maze of town-behind-town.

At night, drunk on the cold, Muna will dunk
candy bars in hot chocolate
as we sit on wool blankets, while boys eat pizza

and watch cartoons at another table. For now, the road,
generous with awe and rut, continues
to be our road. The trees thin into fields, swell into

cloudy fields of pink tsampa, clouds of pink
swelling, wide squares abundant, rich, fairytale
flowerheads blooming pink. Pink

on pink. Prayer flags flap on poles above
in particular order, and the monk explains
their colors to me. I wonder

how to exist on multiple earths
responsibly. He answers my very many questions
then we laugh at YouTube videos. The road

closes up again ahead. Men are racing horses.
Arcs of fine dust kick up
and the day is fading. The driver's patience

is also fading. He needs to deliver
these goddamn punchy onions. But
the lone man standing to block the road

from traffic to protect the riders
shakes his head. So we clamber onto broad, dusk-lit rocks
beside women as men ride below us. I am a blade

of unused womb, wanting to be a woman
watching men ride, wanting to be a man
riding for the women watching. That guard

wanders off. Our driver beckons us back and we speed past
the horses and their riders until we are sure no one
will catch us. The road to Manang

ends with us on a sun-bleached
wood bench, under clouds shredding
and collecting thin skins. I am far. Muna touches

my cheeks. Her touch
closes the distance between myself
and myself. We split whiskey and still ourselves under

a giddy moon silvering
in a pink sky. We're alive, acutely,
and we're alive beside each other.

Oh, I say, and she *hmmms*. Is that sky.

2. An Elegy for T., Who I Saw with Us
as We Traveled Back from Manang above the River

I went to a place in the world
that's never seen you, T.
Or maybe by now you've seen all places.

Maybe the wet jeweled rocks
have already loosened under your palms,
your palms smoothed

by daylight, by nightfall, by the inarticulable
largeness of time. Bigger than I
can be in this body. I imagined you—

from the jerky clutch—perched
on the wet black boulder, arms
gleaming around your naked knees, mist-washed,

your toes and soles gripping, your gaze
forward, past, elsewhere, your gaze
with us, with us, outside

time, outside the river. This is not wintertime
in Harlem. I am not kissing your cheek goodbye
while snow clings to our eyelashes. Up here the light is damp.

The rock-pocked mud. Trees shuddering
when we roll over their roots—
damp. The waterfalls that wet the air

before they're visible, damp. The mist is
                 profuse: I delicate echo your hand,
          silly sobbing crows.

T., I'm learning that I can avoid
what I love until one of us is gone,
swept and taken, made adrift, or worn

into a new shape. I love you
here too: I love
you here. You are all the lifting rushing, each of the rivers.

Love is so queer, so unreasonably permanent.
I imagine the mist drew you
as it drew us, like a dream quivering

just out of frame. Quivering
with a sound that seals it, a sound
that rises from the river that knows and makes you.

You: gleaming root
of a woman, shining branched tree
of a woman, us traveling

alongside and within you, far
from any dirt I know as home.
Not mine, none of it mine. Not even my body is mine,

a visitation. A cosmos. Imagining next to another,
her also a cosmos. You a cosmos. The river twisting
and washing below. How anchoring,

our sounding together,
bouncing along, imagining
life after life. Cosmos, seed, species

inventando. We're
sound. Sing it
forward, backward,   all time, no time at all.

NOTES

On a hot July night in La Fábrica in Havana, a woman said to me, in Spanish, "It must be difficult in your liberation struggle [in norteamérica/the US] to imagine you are not part of las américas." Her phrasing gifted me the possibility of imagining the US, and those of us now within the US, as part of las américas. Her concern—for our peoples' feeling of being separated by the geography of empire, for internalizing this separation even as multiple liberation struggles take flight throughout our hemisphere—moved me. Adjacent questions underwrite this book: What about the Bronx, as an isolated, rich, embedded geography within las américas? What can it mean to exist in a violently-invented set of nations? How am I complicit in this violence even as I am subject to it? If our species is bent on dreaming and invention, how might one make a different dream?

Cover

The sculpture on the cover is from the artist Gabriela Salazar's 2018 project *Matters in Shelter (and Place, Puerto Rico)*. On materiality, from that exhibition statement: "Concrete is a building material increasingly necessary in Puerto Rico for its resiliency against dangerous tropical storms and hurricanes, but is itself one of the leading causes of climate change due to the significant carbon emissions generated in its production. Other blocks are made of an unstable, homemade, coffee-based clay. The artist's mother grew up on a coffee farm in Puerto Rico, and coffee had been resurgent in Puerto Rican agriculture—gains that were decimated by Hurricane Maria. As the coffee blocks disintegrate, the artist will replenish them. Salazar has said, 'The process of making the coffee clay is central to the work: repeating the manual labor in it, and the Sisyphean attempt to make a thing that you know is going to fall apart.'"

Epigraph

Sylvia Wynter's "We must now collectively undertake a rewriting of
knowledge as we know it" is published in an interview by Katherine
McKittrick in *Sylvia Wynter: On Being Human as Praxis*.

Our América Is Botanic

The poem that begins with "On a yellow bus" draws three lines —"She had
horses who danced in her mother's arms. / She had horses who thought they
were the sun and their / bodies shone like stars"— from Joy Harjo's poem
"She Had Some Horses."

Uptown Summers

This sequence attempts to observe the zuihitsu form as Kimiko Hahn
describes it in *The Narrow Road to the Interior*: as both "encompassing" and
having a "sense of disorder that feels so integral." Cheryl Boyce-Taylor's
zuihitsus, and her teaching of them, led me to Hahn's work and then to
make this poem.

Radical Imagining Is Our Evolutionary Project

In a seed shop in Arizona, Saretta Morgan and I lit upon the idea of the
human body as an archive that is not unlike a seed. Elsewhere, Gabrielle
Calvocoressi taught me about violets and syntactical saturation.

Toni Morrison calls racism "a profound neurosis" in her May 7, 1993, interview with Charlie Rose. Her framing aligns with my wondering/positioning of racism here as an affliction that lends itself to neurosis and/or psychosis not always visible to the self (anosognosia). In the biopic *Toni Morrison: The Pieces I Am*, Morrison, delighted, flicks white gaze off of her shoulder.

The line "thrown up against a sharp white background" is Zora Neale Hurston's, from her 1928 essay *How It Feels to be Colored Me*, which Glen Ligon stenciled in oil over and over as the words disappeared and smudged into a new configuration in his 1990 piece *Untitled*.

An important reference for me on haunting is Marisa Parham's *Haunting and Displacement in African American Literature and Culture*.

Deliberately and With Such Love Archive the Holdings

Manang is in Nepal. During summer 2018, I visited Muna Gurung in Kathmandu. We traveled to the town of Manang and back to Kathmandu together.

I love Trishon Crawford—who left this (which?) world in 2016—very much.

ACKNOWLEDGMENTS

My deepest gratitude to the editors, curators, and artists who published earlier or current versions of the work in *Future Botanic* in these spaces:

The Academy of American Poets
Apogee Journal
Aster(ix) Journal
Bettering American Poetry Volume 2
The Center for Book Arts
Four Way Review
Hayden's Ferry Review
Lincoln Center's "We Are the Work"
Mantis: A Journal of Poetry, Criticism, and Translation
No, Dear, issue 18: *#BlackPoetsSpeakOut*
The Rumpus

A massive, loving thank-you to the extraordinary people who have offered support (gifts of time, of audience, of funding, and/or of community) via these institutions and programs:

Asian American Writers Workshop
Bowery Poetry Cafe
Calypso Muse
The Center for Book Arts
Community Art Works
Easton's Nook
The Frost Place
Girls Write Now
The Jerome Foundation
Lower Manhattan Cultural Council
Nomadic Coffee

One Breath Rising
The Poetry Project
Soul Sister Revue
SupaDupaFresh

Thank you to Roberto Carlos Garcia—such tremendous heart, soul, and intelligence you bring to your commitment to our community and to our work together—and also to the brilliant and wonderful Kayla Reyes and Natalia Carmalengo of Get Fresh Books Publishing—for making a beautiful home for *Future Botanic.* Mad love.

Thank you to Mahogany L. Browne, Ama Codjoe, Natalie Diaz, Abou Farman, Ricardo Maldonado, Yesenia Montilla, Carina del Valle Schorske, KMA Sullivan, and Andrea Warmack for your time, generosity, and critical feedback on drafts of this book. I am so grateful for you and for us.

Thank you to Emilie Boone, Gabrielle Civil, Carol Crawford, Zaqia Crawford, LaTasha N. Nevada Diggs, Jasmin Dendariarena, Aricka Foreman, Cristina Maria Fort Garces, Katrina Gonzales, Rajib Guha, Muna Gurung, Rosamond King, Muriel Leung, Saretta Morgan, Toby Nathan, Natasha Michelle Norton, the Olivares clan, Marisa Parham, Seema Reza, Peggy Robles-Alvarado, Purvi Shah, Althea Stevens, and Tachira Tavarez. Our kinships and conversations enabled this project in radically different ways, and I am so grateful for each of you.

For your wisdom, humor, and openheartedness in our writing groups, thank you to Cheryl Clarke, LeConte Dill, and Ellen Hagan; and to Cheryl Boyce-Taylor, E.J. Antonio, JP Howard, and Caits Meissner.

Les adoro.

AUTHOR BIO

Christina Olivares is the author of *No Map of the Earth Includes Stars*, winner of the 2014 Marsh Hawk Press Book Prize, and of the chaplet *Interrupt* (Belladonna★ Collaborative, 2015). Olivares is an educator, is a poverty and prison abolitionist, and identifies as queer American-Cuban. Olivares is proud to be from the Bronx.